Systems of Government

THEOCRACY
Religious Government

SYSTEMS OF GOVERNMENT

Systems of Government

THEOCRACY
Religious Government

Tara Derrick

MASON CREST
PHILADELPHIA

Mason Crest
450 Parkway Drive, Suite D
Broomall, PA 19008
www.masoncrest.com

© 2019 by Mason Crest, an imprint of National Highlights, Inc.

Printed and bound in the United States of America.

CPSIA Compliance Information: Batch #GOV2018.
For further information, contact Mason Crest at 1-866-MCP-Book.

First printing
1 3 5 7 9 8 6 4 2

Library of Congress Cataloging-in-Publication Data

Names: Derrick, Tara, author.
Title: Theocracy : religious government / Tara Derrick.
Description: Philadelphia : Mason Crest Publishers, 2019. | Series: Systems
  of government | Includes bibliographical references and index.
Identifiers: LCCN 2017058172 (print) | LCCN 2017052201 (ebook) | ISBN
  9781422277744 (ebook) | ISBN 9781422240229 (hc)
Subjects: LCSH: Theocracy—Juvenile literature.
Classification: LCC JC372 (print) | LCC JC372 .D47 2019 (ebook) | DDC
  321/.5—dc23
LC record available at https://lccn.loc.gov/2017058172

Systems of Government series ISBN: 978-1-4222-4014-4

QR CODES AND LINKS TO THIRD-PARTY CONTENT

4

Table of Contents

KEY ICONS TO LOOK FOR:

Words to understand: These words with their easy-to-understand definitions will increase the reader's understanding of the text while building vocabulary skills.

Sidebars: This boxed material within the main text allows readers to build knowledge, gain insights, explore possibilities, and broaden their perspectives by weaving together additional information to provide realistic and holistic perspectives.

Educational Videos: Readers can view videos by scanning our QR codes, providing them with additional educational content to supplement the text. Examples include news coverage, moments in history, speeches, iconic sports moments and much more!

Text-dependent questions: These questions send the reader back to the text for more careful attention to the evidence presented there.

Research projects: Readers are pointed toward areas of further inquiry connected to each chapter. Suggestions are provided for projects that encourage deeper research and analysis.

Series glossary of key terms: This back-of-the-book glossary contains terminology used throughout this series. Words found here increase the reader's ability to read and comprehend higher-level books and articles in this field.

Afghan women walk past a mosque in the city of Mazar-e-Sharif. From 1996 until 2001, Afghanistan was ruled by a fundamentalist organization called the Taliban. The Taliban insisted that all people follow Islamic laws, including ones that required women to wear garments that covered them from head to toe when in public.

 Words to Understand in This Chapter

burqa—a loose, shapeless garment for women that covers the entire body and is worn in some conservative Muslim countries.

polytheism—the worshiping of many gods.

Quran—Islam's holy scriptures.

Sharia—Islamic law, based primarily on the Quran and the Sunna, the teachings and practices of the Prophet Muhammad.

1 Rule by God

Kamila Yastali wasn't a police officer or a fire-fighter, but she nevertheless risked her life each day she worked. Behind the walls of her modest home in Kabul, the capital of Afghanistan, Yastali ran an illegal school. If the authorities uncovered her clandestine operation, she could be hanged.

Yastali's pupils also risked harsh punishment, for they too were breaking the law. To avoid attracting attention, they always arrived singly at their instructor's house, and they never congregated with one another or lingered on the streets of the middle-class neighborhood after the day's illicit lessons were done.

The stealth might seem appropriate for a spy ring. But Yastali wasn't training her students in the techniques of espi-

Key Idea

In a theocracy, religious law is supreme. The government enforces the moral and social values of the dominant religion.

onage, assassination, or sabotage. Her lessons were in math and science, literature and languages. What made the school illegal was that the students and their teacher were female. Shortly after coming to power in 1996, Afghanistan's ruling group—known as the Taliban—had issued an edict banning formal education for girls over the age of nine. The Taliban government also prohibited women from being teachers.

These restrictions, the Taliban claimed, were not simply in the best interests of women. They were necessary to bring Afghan society into conformance with the will of God. All behavior—private as well as public—was to be regulated by Islam, at least as the Taliban interpreted the religion's dictates. Afghanistan was, in short, a theocracy.

"Ascribing the Power to God"

The English word *theocracy* is derived from two Greek terms: *theos*, meaning "god"; and *kratein*, "to rule." So theocracy literally means "rule by God." That, of course, is much too vague to serve as a useful definition. A working definition of theocracy might be a government that 1) claims divine guidance or is regarded as being divinely guided; and 2) uses the power of the state to enforce conformity to religious rules or laws.

Theocracy is quite old. In one form or another, this type of government has existed since at least 3100 BCE. But the first known description of theocracy dates to about 97 CE. "Some

A young Afghan girl reads aloud to her class in a rural area near Kabul. The Islamist religious group known as the Taliban destroyed the school where these girls once studied and prohibited young women from getting an education.

A statue of the Biblical leader Moses holding stone tablets that represent the Ten Commandments, the central principles of Judaism. The ancient Hebrew community is an example of a theocracy.

legislators have permitted their governments to be under monarchies," the Jewish historian Josephus wrote in *Against Apion*, "others put them under oligarchies, and others under a republican form; but our legislator [Moses] . . . ordained our government to be what, by a strained expression, may be termed a theocracy, by ascribing the authority and the power to God."

Josephus was trying to explain (and defend) Judaism to a Roman audience. Theocracy stood outside his readers' frame of reference. In the classical world, governments were categorized according to terms set forth by the Greek philosopher Aristotle (384–322 BCE). Aristotle identified three forms of government (government by one person, government by a few people, and government by many people). Each of these forms had a pure and a corrupted variation, for a total of six possible government types. Thus, government by one person could be a monarchy (in which a virtuous king governs for the benefit of all of society) or a tyranny (an individual ruling for his own gain). Government by a few could be aristocracy (rule by the best, in the interest of all) or oligarchy (rule by the rich and well born, for their own gain). Government by many could be a polity, or constitutional republic (with citizens taking turns governing, for the benefit of all) or a democracy (in which all citizens voted directly, which Aristotle thought would lead to the masses of poor people acting for their own gain). In every case, the key factor was the person or persons exercising governing power, the actual rulers. In the theocracy Josephus described—a theocracy that would have existed perhaps 1,500 years before his time—the governing power lay with God, who

Muslims participate in Friday prayers at a mosque in Isfahan, Iran. Since 1979, a council of Islamic religious leaders has ruled Iran, making it one of the world's few theocracies today.

wasn't physically present among the people. Moses led the Jewish people, but only as God's representative.

In the Bible account, Moses communicates directly with God. He relays God's instructions (as, for example, when he carries down from Mount Sinai the stone tablets on which God has inscribed the Ten Commandments).

In Islam, Muhammad ibn Abdullah plays a similar role as God's intermediary. Muhammad was a merchant in Mecca, a city on the Arabian Peninsula. Beginning in 610 CE, he reported a series of divine revelations. In those revelations, the angel

Gabriel dictates God's words, which Muhammad is commanded to share with other people. The revelations form the *Quran*, Islam's holy scripture. Its content is quite varied. One important theme is the nature of God. Another is how people should live and worship properly.

In 622, Muhammad's followers—known as Muslims—were forced to leave Mecca. They settled about 200 miles to the north, in the oasis town of Yathrib. There, under Muhammad's leadership, the first Muslim state was established.

Variations

The stories of Muhammad and Moses illustrate one way theocracy has historically found expression: in the form of a govern-

 Common Definitions of Theocracy

Theocracy, which can take a variety of forms, is difficult to define in a comprehensive way. The following are only some of the accepted definitions of theocracy:

- a state ruled directly or indirectly by clergy (for example, priests, ministers, or mullahs)
- a state in which civil law is the same as religious law
- a government that requires citizens' social behavior to conform to religious law
- government by a leader who is believed to be a god or the human representative of God
- government by a person who claims to communicate directly with God and to relay God's instructions to the community.

ment whose leader claims to have direct communication with God and claims to be relaying or revealing God's instructions to humanity. But theocracy is a diverse phenomenon. It has taken other forms as well.

For example, theocracies may arise in the absence of a living prophet. Islamic theocratic states were established in Iran and Afghanistan in the late 20th century, more than 1,300 years after the death of Muhammad. Jesus lived in the first century CE, but Christian reformers founded theocracies, among other places, in Switzerland during the 1550s and the Massachusetts Bay Colony during the 1630s. In cases such as these, scripture tends to be cited as justification for "rule by God."

Where *polytheism* (belief in multiple gods) exists, a different form of theocracy has sometimes arisen. Leaders have claimed to be, or have been regarded, as gods in their own right. Such leaders don't merely relay or interpret the divine will. As god-kings, they are part of the sacred realm. Thus, in theory

Educational Video

To watch a short video on theocracy, scan here:

The Word Theocracy Comes From The Greek Word Theokratia, Which Is A Compound Word That Combines Theos, Which Means God, And Kratein, Which Means To Rule

their decisions as rulers are above reproach by their human subjects.

Common Features

Variations aside, all theocracies have certain common characteristics. First, they occur only in societies in which a significant portion of the people believe in the existence of God or of multiple gods. For obvious reasons, a theocracy cannot be sustained among an atheistic population.

Key Quote

"Theocratic, or to make the Lord God our Governour is the best form of Government in a Christian Common-wealth, and which men that are free to chuse . . . ought to establish."

—John Davenport, cofounder of New Haven Colony (1639)

But theocracy also requires a specific kind of religious outlook—namely, the assumption that human affairs and human conduct are matters of interest to the Almighty. It's possible to believe in God while denying any divine presence or influence in the material world. The Deists of the 18th century, for example, said that God created the universe and its physical laws, then simply set everything in motion, never intervening in any way thereafter. These kinds of beliefs will never give rise to a theocracy. Theocratic regimes enforce conformity to rules regarded as divinely ordained. A God who stands completely apart from humanity is a God who doesn't reveal laws people must follow, and who neither rewards nor punishes humans for their behavior.

The idea of divine judgment is important in all theocracies. The way that judgment is understood, however, varies. Premodern cultures tend to view pleasing the gods as a collective responsibility, with consequences for all of society. If the gods are given their due, they will bestow rewards on society, or at the very least not interfere with its smooth functioning. But if people's behavior offends them, the gods will visit punishment on society. This typically takes the form of a natural disaster (for example, a failed harvest, disease epidemic, or earthquake) or a military defeat.

In modern societies, by contrast, it is more often assumed that any divine reward or punishment accrues to individuals, and for their own behavior. It is also commonly held that God punishes or rewards a person in the afterlife rather than during his or her earthly existence. Despite this, modern theocratic regimes don't give individuals free rein to make their own moral decisions. Instead, these regimes attempt to make everyone in the society follow the dictates of the dominant religion (as interpreted by the religious leaders who control the regime).

Modern theocratic governments have used various means to ensure religious conformity. Many have attempted to eliminate opposing viewpoints by controlling the educational system, by censoring the media, or by limiting citizens' contact with outsiders. Some theocratic regimes have expelled dissenters. That tactic was used by the Puritans of Massachusetts Bay Colony, and by the Latter-day Saints of Utah Territory during the second half of the 19th century. Other theocracies have resorted to far more coercive measures. The Taliban employed roaming "morality police" who beat, flogged, and sometimes even killed Afghanis found in violation of the regime's strict version of *Sharia*, or Islamic law. Offenders included men whose beards were too short; women seen in public not covered from head to toe in a *burqa* and accompanied by a male relative; and anyone dancing or playing music. Saudi Arabia's morality police, called

Powerful storms and other destructive natural events were probably interpreted by early humans as representing the anger of the gods. Theocratic governments arose in part from a belief that humans could appease the gods and therefore prevent natural disasters from devastating their communities.

Saudi Arabian police guard the Ka'aba, the holiest Islamic shrine, while Muslim pilgrims visiting the city of Mecca walk past. In Saudi Arabia, special police called mutaween make sure that all people are following the moral laws imposed by the country's theocratic government.

mutaween, play a similar role in rooting out "un-Islamic" conduct in that nation.

An Outmoded Form of Government?

Theocracies have existed, at one time or another, all over the globe. And they have been spawned by a variety of creeds. Under certain conditions, almost any religion can give rise to a theocratic regime.

Nevertheless, theocracy has historically been a relatively rare form of government. And today it is viewed as outmoded in much, if not most, of the world. In Western societies especially, theocracy also tends to be seen in a wholly negative light. It is regarded as a repressive form of government, one that inevitably infringes on the basic right of individuals to hold whatever religious beliefs they choose.

Needless to say, not everybody living under a theocracy would agree. Government enforcement of piety may be seen as desirable in societies in which a large majority of the population follows the same religion, and the religion in question is understood to include absolute rules of human conduct.

Theocracy can thus promote social cohesion. There is little doubt it served that function in certain ancient cultures.

 Text-Dependent Questions

1. What group of strict Islamic fundamentalists ruled Afghanistan from 1996 until 2001?
2. What is the meaning of the word *theocracy*?
3. What are some of the common characteristics of all theocracies?

 Research Project

Using your school library or the internet, research some other forms of government, such as monarchy, oligarchy, or communism. What are some ways that these forms of government are different from democracy? Are there ways that they are the same? Make a list and share it with your class.

In the Roman Empire from the first century BCE *until the fourth century* CE, *Augustus and other leaders were worshiped as gods.*

 Words to Understand in This Chapter

chaos—complete disorder and confusion.

legitimacy—justification to govern.

pantheon—the term given to all of the gods worshiped or believed in by the people of a particular region or country.

phenomena—facts, occurrences, or circumstances that can be observed, especially those that are impressive or extraordinary.

2 Ancient Theocracies

In earlier times, natural *phenomena* such as floods, famine, the rising of the sun, and eclipses of the moon were attributed to supernatural beings or gods. Ancient peoples developed special rituals to please the gods and keep their communities safe. In some societies, people also believed that their king had special abilities to communicate with and influence the gods. When civil and religious authority was combined in the hands of one person, a strong theocratic government resulted.

Theocracy may have been fairly common among ancient societies. However, in all but a handful of cases, the archaeological record is very limited (or is nonexistent), so definitive conclusions can't be made.

Only a few ancient theocracies have been studied in depth. The ancient Egyptian civilization flourished for nearly three millennia in northeastern Africa. It left an abundance of written records and other artifacts from which scholars have been able to piece together the workings of the Egyptian theocracy, which was headed by the powerful pharaohs. In the Western Hemisphere, the Maya, Aztecs, and Inca also had powerful theocratic rulers. Knowledge of these theocracies comes not only from archaeology but also from accounts written after the Spanish conquests of the 16th century.

Many details about the Egyptian, Mayan, Aztec, and Incan theocracies may never be known. Still, scholars understand the broad outlines. As with all theocratic regimes, what gave the Egyptian, Mayan, Aztec, and Incan rulers *legitimacy* was their supposed special relationship with the gods. But the Egyptian pharaohs, the Mayan kings, and the Aztec and Incan emperors were more than just representatives of the gods on earth. They were more than intermediaries between the divine and human realms. They were god-kings. When crowned, these rulers were thought to become divine.

Theocracy in Ancient Egypt

The Nile, the world's longest river, cuts through the vast and forbidding deserts of Egypt. The river's life-sustaining waters attracted human settlers from as early as 7000 BCE. Agriculture began in the Nile Valley some 2,000 years later. Farming was made possible by the river's regular flooding, which deposited (usually each year) a new layer of nutrient-rich soil on the surrounding land.

The falcon-headed god Horus is carved onto the side of an ancient temple at Luxor, Egypt.

Ramesses the Great ruled Egypt during the 13th century BCE. *In ancient Egypt, the pharaohs were believed to be divine, and their decrees could not be challenged.*

By the fourth millennium BCE, Lower Egypt (the Nile Delta region) and Upper Egypt (the area to the south) were controlled by two separate kingdoms. Around 3100 a ruler from Upper Egypt—probably Narmer—conquered Lower Egypt and united the two kingdoms. Narmer is generally credited with founding Egypt's first dynasty of pharaohs. Scholars believe that from his reign until 332 BCE, when Egypt was conquered by Alexander the Great of Macedon, there were a total of 31 dynasties.

Worship of the gods influenced all activities and all classes of people in ancient Egypt. The gods were believed to control the sun, the moon, the earth, the sky, and the Nile River. All of these natural forces had to be kept happy. Two of the most important gods in the Egyptian *pantheon* were Horus and Osiris. Horus—usually depicted as a man with the head of a falcon—ruled over the sky, including the sun and the moon. Osiris, the green-skinned father of Horus, was god of the afterlife. He judged the souls of the dead. He also had another important function: to bring rebirth to the earth through the sprouting of plants in the spring. Osiris was a symbol of resurrection and eternal life.

In the Egyptian theocracy, Horus and Osiris both became associated with the pharaohs. When a pharaoh was crowned, the spirit of Horus was believed to enter him, making the pharaoh divine. The pharaoh served as an intermediary between his people and the gods, maintaining order and preventing *chaos* in Egypt. As a god he was considered infallible. When he settled disputes or made legal judgments, his decision could not be questioned. There was no standard written law.

All justice depended on the decisions of the pharaoh.

During his lifetime, the pharaoh was worshiped at temples. He continued to be worshiped even after death. Pharaohs participated in all major religious festivals. Two of the most important were Heb-Sed and Opet. The Heb-Sed Festival was held after a pharaoh had reigned for 30 years, and it was celebrated every three years after that. The purpose of Heb-Sed was to restore the pharaoh's strength and ritually acknowledge his continuing right to rule. The Opet Festival was probably first held near the beginning of the 18th dynasty (ca. 1550 BCE). It celebrated the marriage of two gods, but also reinforced the idea of the pharaoh's divinity through a re-coronation ceremony.

Upon death, the pharaoh's spirit was believed to merge with the god Osiris and gain eternal life. In his eternal life in the underworld, the pharaoh would continue to protect the people of his kingdom. This made a proper burial very important and led to the building of the Great Pyramids and complex burial chambers carved out of cliffs along the Nile River. Meanwhile, the dynasty continued with the crowning of a new pharaoh.

Not surprisingly, the religious beliefs of the ancient Egyptians evolved somewhat over the course of centuries. The importance of specific gods waxed or waned. New gods were sometimes added to the pantheon.

But one pharaoh made a radical break with traditional Egyptian religion. That pharaoh, Akhenaten, took the throne around 1353 BCE. Within a few years, he had replaced the worship of many gods with the worship of only one: Aten, the disk

Educational Video

To learn more about the government of ancient Egypt, scan here:

of the sun. After Akhenaten's death, his son Tutankhamun restored polytheism to Egypt.

Another aspect of ancient Egypt's theocracy deserves special mention. In about a half-dozen instances, women reigned as pharaohs. Female leaders—under any political system—were quite uncommon until modern times. In theocratic systems, women almost never rule, though there is also evidence for a few female rulers among the Maya.

Mayan Theocracy

The Maya began farming in southern Mexico and northern Central America around 5000 BCE. By 2000 BCE, they were living in small city-states, each with its own hereditary king. Unlike the ancient Egyptians (or the Aztecs and the Inca), the Maya never developed a large, centralized empire. Instead, the city-state remained the primary political unit of Mayan civilization up to the time of the Spanish conquest.

The various Mayan city-states formed alliances. Some

sought to extend their influence or attain regional dominance through diplomacy. The city-states also fought frequent wars. For much of Mayan history, however, these wars were limited in scope. Fighting was confined to soldiers, and the main objective was to take enemy prisoners—including, if possible, the king. The prisoners would later be sacrificed to the gods. Conquerors typically demanded tribute, but they didn't destroy defeated city-states. Civilians were thus minimally affected by warfare.

Mayan culture reached its peak during the era archaeologists call the Classic Period, which lasted roughly from 250 CE to

 ## Native American Ball Game

The Maya and Aztecs, as well as other cultures in Mesoamerica, played a ball game that often had religious significance. The game took place on an I-shaped court that was usually bounded by sloping stone walls. The object was to hit a heavy rubber ball—without using hands or feet and without allowing the ball to come to a stop—over a center line to the opposing team's side. In some versions, knocking the ball through a high ring meant automatic victory.

The ball game was sometimes played just for recreation or entertainment. But it was also played as part of religious rituals. Among some Mayan groups, the game may have served as a reenactment of episodes from a creation myth. For the Aztecs, the game may have symbolized the struggle between Huitzilopochtli (god of the sun) and the gods of the night.

The outcome of a ball game could have serious consequences for the players. Human sacrifices were sometimes conducted in conjunction with a game, and some scholars suggest that the victims might have included the captain of the losing team.

900 CE. During the Classic Period, the Maya created stunning works of art and architecture, including massive stepped pyramids that were used in religious ceremonies and, sometimes, as tombs for kings. The Maya were accomplished astronomers. They correctly calculated the length of a year as 365.25 days. They also excelled in mathematics, using the concept of zero long before it was understood in Europe, for example.

The Maya worshiped many gods associated with nature, but beyond that their religious beliefs were complex. In the Mayan view, the universe was divided into three planes: the Heavens, the Earth, and the Underworld, also known as the Place of Awe. The Underworld, which could be reached through caves and subterranean rivers, was inhabited by a host of terrifying gods and demons. Mayan religious ceremonies—some of which included ritual human sacrifice—were supposed to keep those malignant beings from coming up to the earthly plane. Other ceremonies were performed to please the more benign gods, so that they would help the community. These gods included the Rain God, the Maize God, and the Sun God.

Like the pharaohs of Egypt, Mayan rulers were considered god-kings. They served as intermediaries between their human subjects and the gods. Mayan kings regularly offered their own blood to satisfy the gods. These bloodletting ceremonies involved excruciating pain. For example, one method of drawing blood was to pull a rope of thorns through the tongue.

Besides the god-kings who ruled the city-states, Mayan theocracy featured an important class of priests. They fore-

The ancient Mayan ruins at Tikal, Guatemala, include the Temple of the Great Jaguar, which was the burial place of a Mayan ruler. It was built around 700 CE and is more than 150 feet high.

cast—based largely on the interactions between the Maya's 260-day sacred calendar and the 365-day civil calendar—when the time was favorable for various endeavors. These included military campaigns, royal weddings, religious ceremonies, and the like.

Toward the end of the Classic Period, Mayan civilization began to crumble in many if not all places. Temples and monuments stopped being built. Important Mayan cities were abandoned completely. Scholars aren't certain what caused this cultural breakdown. Many theories have been offered. One is that agricultural production collapsed because of a long drought or unsustainable farming practices. Another blames a shift toward total warfare, with enemies targeting each other's civilian populations. Still another theory suggests that ordinary people lost faith in the legitimacy of their theocratic rulers, perhaps because of some catastrophe. A combination of factors may well have been at work.

Whatever the case, the Maya never again reached the same heights of cultural achievement. The Mayan civilization that the Spanish conquistadors encountered in the early 1500s was well past its prime.

Aztec and Inca

In contrast to the Maya, the Aztec and Incan civilizations were both at their height when the conquistadors arrived. The Aztecs dominated central Mexico. The Inca controlled much of western South America.

Both civilizations excelled in engineering and building. The Aztecs, for example, built their capital, Tenochtitlán, in the middle of a lake. The Inca constructed cities and an extensive road network high up in the rugged Andes Mountains.

The Aztecs and the Inca were both warlike peoples. Each carved out a large empire in a relatively short period of time. The first Inca ruler, Manco Capac, built a capital at Cuzco (in present-day Peru) in the early 13th century CE. It wasn't until about 1400, however, that the Inca began conquering neighboring peoples. In little more than a century, they had created an empire that was some 2,500 miles long and 500 miles wide.

The Aztecs, a small tribe of unknown origin, wandered into the Valley of Mexico during the late 12th or early 13th century. Tenochtitlán was founded in 1325, but construction of the city's causeways, canals, and monumental temples and pyramids required generations to complete. Until 1430, the Aztecs were dominated by another people, called the Tepanecs. Joining with two other city-states, the Aztecs overthrew Tepanec rule and founded an empire. Conquests during the next 90 years expanded the empire to the Atlantic and Pacific coasts. The empire was ruled by the Huey Tlatoani, or Great Speaker. He was worshiped as a god and had absolute power.

According to Aztec beliefs, Huitzilopochtli—the god of war and the sun—was engaged in a never-ending struggle with gods associated with the moon and stars. Huitzilopochtli required a vast supply of life-energy to sustain him in this struggle. Otherwise, the gods of the night would prevail. The sun wouldn't rise, and the world would be plunged into perpetual darkness. To provide Huitzilopochtli with life-energy, the Aztecs carried out human sacrifice on a massive scale. Victims—usually prisoners of war or people from conquered groups sent to

This colossal stone representation of Tlaloc, the god of rain, can today be seen today near Mexico City, where the Aztec capital, Tenochtitlán, was once located.

Tenochtitlán as tribute—would be taken to the top of a pyramid. The victim's arms and legs would be held down as an Aztec priest cut open the chest, pulled out the still-beating heart, and offered it to Huitzilopochtli. (Human sacrifices were offered to other gods as well.)

Apart from the religious belief that they kept the world from collapsing into darkness, the Aztec sacrifices would have served a couple of political goals. The sacrifices certainly intimidated conquered peoples. They also reinforced the godlike authority of the Huey Tlatoani.

The Inca also practiced human sacrifice, but not nearly on the same scale as the Aztecs. Inca sacrificial victims were often children taken to a mountain peak, where they died of exposure. After death they were believed to become divine and to act as oracles, communicating messages from the gods.

Incan religion involved worship of many gods, as well as sacred places. Like the Aztec Huey Tlatoani, the Inca emperor—called the Sapa Inca ("Great Inca")—was considered a god. He was believed to be a direct descendant of Inti, the god of the sun. The Sapa Inca's person was so sacred that he was carried everywhere on a golden litter so that his feet wouldn't be profaned by touching the ground. All objects that the Sapa Inca touched were collected and ritually burned. This was to prevent ordinary people from touching anything that had come into contact with the god-king.

* * * * *

When a ruler is believed to be a god—like the Huey Tlatoani or the Sapa Inca—his subjects are likely to display extraordinary obedience and loyalty. This sort of theocratic

This monumental Aztec sculpture, known as the Sun Stone, includes a representation of the sun god at the center, holding human hearts in each hand and with a sacrificial knife in place of his tongue.

government, history shows, can lead to highly cohesive societies. On the other hand, these societies can easily be paralyzed if their leader is incapacitated or the limits of his actual power are exposed. Peoples accustomed to following a ruler without question often founder when a need for independent decision making suddenly arises.

This is well illustrated by the Spanish conquests of the Aztecs and Inca. In November 1519, the Spanish conquistador Hernán Cortés entered Tenochtitlán at the invitation of the Aztec ruler, Moctezuma II. Cortés had about 150 Spanish sol-

The Inca city of Machu Picchu was located above the Urubamba Valley of Peru, a region considered sacred by the Inca people.

diers under his command, while the population of Moctezuma's capital is thought to have numbered several hundred thousand. But when Cortés made Moctezuma a captive in his own palace, Aztec society—including a mighty army that had vanquished numerous enemies—remained paralyzed for months.

The results were similar when the Spanish conquistador Francisco Pizarro met the Sapa Inca, Atahuallpa, at Cajamarca in November 1532. Pizarro's force numbered just 168, while an estimated 80,000 Inca warriors were encamped around Cajamarca. Yet Pizarro threw the Inca army into complete disarray after pulling Atahuallpa down from his gilded litter.

 Text-Dependent Questions

1. Why do modern scholars not know much about ancient theocracies?
2. What ancient Egyptian ruler united the kingdoms of Upper Egypt and Lower Egypt around 3100 BCE?
3. How did the Aztecs provide their god Huitzilopochtli with life-energy to sustain him in a conflict with the moon and star gods?

 Research Project

Using your school library or the internet, find out more about the Egyptian pantheon of deities. Choose one of the Egyptian gods—such as Osiris, Horus, Anubis, Set, or another deity—and find out more about this god. Write a two-page report and share it with your class.

Muslim pilgrims gather outside al-Masjid al-Nabawi (the Mosque of the Prophet) in Medina, Saudi Arabia. The Prophet Muhammad, who first preached the Islamic religion in the early seventh century, is buried under the green dome. In Medina, Muhammad created the first state ruled by Islamic law during the seventh century CE.

 Words to Understand in This Chapter

caliph—a successor to the Prophet Muhammad as spiritual and temporal leader of the Muslim community.

cleric—a religious leader such as a priest, minister, pastor, imam, mullah, or rabbi.

coup—the sudden overthrow of a government by a small group, often through violent means.

mullah—in Islam, an educated religious leader.

secular—not religious.

3 Islamic Theocracies

Muhammad ibn Abdullah, the Messenger of Allah, was both a prophet and a political leader. Born in 570 in Mecca, Muhammad said he received the first of his revelations from God in 610. At first, he shared the revelations only with a few family members and close friends. In 613, however, Muhammad began sharing God's message publicly. Gradually, a widening circle of people adopted the religion Muhammad preached: Islam.

Many Meccans were hostile toward Muhammad and the small but growing community of Muslims in their midst. Islam's central message is that there is only one God, to whom people must submit (the word *Islam*, in fact, means "submission"). Yet Arabs at the time were polytheistic, and merchants made a lot of money catering to the pilgrims who flocked to Mecca to worship the idols in a shrine called the Ka'aba. Muhammad also took Mecca's wealthy and powerful to task for their mistreatment of the poor.

Under the threat of violence, Muhammad and several hundred followers left Mecca in 622. They settled in Yathrib. There Muhammad demonstrated his skill as a political leader. He negotiated a pact with the Jewish tribes living in Yathrib. Among other terms, it committed the Jewish tribes and the Muslims to support each other in war. It also set Muhammad up as the final arbiter of all disputes. Yathrib was soon renamed Madinat al-Nabi, meaning "City of the Prophet," in Muhammad's honor. In English the city is usually rendered as Medina.

The Muslims raided Mecca's caravans, and intermittent fighting between the two sides went on for years. Meanwhile, the Muslim community came to dominate Medina as Islam gained converts, and Jewish tribes were expelled (or, in one case, slaughtered for supposedly conspiring to betray the Muslims during a siege by Meccan forces). Medina became a theocracy. Islam, as set forth by Muhammad, didn't simply serve as a guide for individual behavior. It also governed all social relations and was even the foundation of the state. "The Medinan community formed a total framework for state, society, and culture," observes John L. Esposito, a noted scholar of Islam. "It epitomized the Quranic mandate for Muslims as individuals and as a community (*umma*) 'to transform the world itself through action in the world.'"

In many ways, Muslims did transform the world. By 630 they had gained the upper hand on Mecca, and Muhammad and his followers marched unopposed into the city. Most peo-

Educational Video

To learn more about the Prophet Muhammad, scan here:

ple in Mecca converted voluntarily to Islam, and Muhammad established a theocracy there. When the Prophet died in 632, the entire Arabian Peninsula was under the control of Islam. In the century that followed, Islam spread—through conquest and voluntarily adoption—across North Africa and into Spain in the west, and as far as the Indian subcontinent in the east. Islam's realm covered more territory than the Roman Empire at its height. Many early Muslims viewed this as a validation of the essential truth of their religion. And because Islam is an all-encompassing way of life, many believed that their religion couldn't be considered successful in the absence of a flourishing Islamic state.

That attitude persists among a substantial number of Muslims today. In this respect, Islam differs from the world's two other great monotheistic faiths: Judaism and Christianity. For thousands of years, Jews lived as minority communities in countries all over the world. Often they shunned involvement in politics and government. In the case of Christianity, Jesus

The system of Islamic laws known as Sharia is based on the teachings in the Quran, the sacred scriptures of Islam. The Quran is a collection of the messages that Muslims believe Allah gave to Muhammad between 610 and 632 CE.

appears to approve the separation of *secular* and religious authority when he says, "Give to Caesar what is Caesar's, but give to God what is God's."

For many Muslims, however, removing religion from government isn't desirable. "In contrast to the belief in separation of church and state," write John L. Esposito and Dalia Mogahed in *Who Speaks for Islam*, "religion and society and faith and power are closely bound and intertwined in Islam. Throughout much of history, to be a Muslim was not simply to belong to a faith community or mosque but to live in an

Islamic community/state, governed by Islamic law." It is for this reason, some Westerners have argued, that Islam lends itself readily to theocracy. But this view is at best an oversimplification. Of about 50 countries with majority-Muslim populations today, arguably only two qualify as theocracies. Still, when the Gallup World Poll recently surveyed 10 countries with predominantly Muslim populations, in four of those countries—Egypt, Pakistan, Jordan, and Bangladesh—more than half of respondents said that Sharia must be the only source of legislation.

Yet Sharia means different things in different places. Contrary to what many non-Muslims assume, Sharia isn't a set of precise, codified laws—as, for example, the United States Code. Rather, it is set of rules and principles derived primarily from the Quran and the *Sunna* (the recorded customs, habits, and practices of the Prophet Muhammad). These sources date to seventh-century Arabia. Not surprisingly, they don't always address, in specific terms, issues confronting Muslims today. To take but one example, the Quran requires that Muslims (men as well as women) dress modestly. But what exactly does that mean? The Taliban interpreted it to mean that a woman in public must be covered from head to toe, with only her eyes showing. In Iran, by contrast, a woman must cover her hair but not her face.

The Sunni-Shia Rift

Variations in the way Sharia is interpreted lead to another important point. Islam—unlike, for example, Roman Catholicism—lacks an official head or worldwide hierarchy. In

Islam no single figure has the authority to rule definitively on matters of faith.

During his lifetime, Muhammad was such a figure. As God's prophet, he spoke with total authority. According to the Quran, Muhammad was also the "Seal of the Prophets"—that is, the last prophet who would ever appear. Thus, it was understood that he could never be replaced.

Still, someone would have to lead the Muslim umma when Muhammad died. He failed to name a successor, and upon his death controversy arose. Some—who would be called the Sunnis—believed that the *caliph*, or temporal and spiritual head of the *umma*, should be chosen from among Muhammad's closest companions. Others—known as the Shia—thought that succession should be based on blood ties to the Prophet. They believed that Ali bin Abi Talib, Muhammad's cousin, should be caliph. Ultimately the Sunni view prevailed, and the first caliph was Abu Bakr, one of Muhammad's lifelong companions.

Though Ali became the fourth caliph, he—like the previous two Sunni caliphs, Umar and Uthman—was assassinated. The rift between Sunnis and Shia would become permanent after Ali's son Husayn tried to enforce his claim to the caliphate. In 680, at the Battle of Karbala, Husayn and his followers were massacred by forces of the Sunni Ummayad dynasty.

In the ensuing centuries, Shiism would develop some distinctive practices and beliefs. Today, Shia constitute only about 15 percent of all Muslims worldwide, though they form a majority in a few countries, including Iran and Iraq. Some conservative Sunnis regard the Shia as heretics.

Shiite Muslims march in observance of Ashura, a festival held on the 10th day of the Islamic month of Muharram. The solemn festival commemorates the martyrdom of Ali's son Husayn at the Battle of Karbala in 680 CE—a battle that marks the permanent division of Islam into Sunni and Shiite factions.

Saudi Arabia

One country where Sunni-Shia relations are perennially tense is Saudi Arabia. Occupying most of the Arabian Peninsula, this oil-rich kingdom contains Islam's two holiest sites, the Ka'aba in Mecca and the Prophet's Mosque in Medina. While about 10 percent of Saudis are Shia Muslims, the other 90 percent adhere to a very conservative form of Sunni Islam. It is commonly known as Wahhabism, though many Saudis prefer the more generic term *Salafi*. Salafists seek to return Islam to its

In Saudi Arabia, women are required to wear a headscarf and veil, called a niqab, when they are in public.

pure roots, which they define as the way the religion was practiced during the time of Muhammad and his companions and the two generations that followed.

The word *Wahhabism* comes from Muhammad ibn Abd al-Wahhab. He was an 18th-century Islamic religious reformer in Arabia. Abd al-Wahhab railed against what he believed to be the many ways Islam had been corrupted over the centuries. He rejected Shiism as well as Sufism (Islamic mysticism). Abd al-Wahhab allied himself with Muhammad ibn Saud, a tribal ruler from Najb, in the central part of the Arabian Peninsula. In the name of purifying Islam, they embarked on a military campaign. Between the mid-1700s and the early 1800s, much of the peninsula was brought under the control of the Saud dynasty. Eventually, the Islamic Ottoman Empire, based in present-day Turkey, was spurred to take action. An invading force from Egypt wrested control of the Arabian Peninsula from the Saud dynasty.

In the early 1900s, Abdul-Aziz ibn Saud, an ancestor of Muhammad ibn Saud, began reconquering the Arabian

Peninsula. He completed that work in 1932, proclaiming the Kingdom of Saudi Arabia. King Abdul-Aziz didn't forget his family's centuries-long connection with Wahhabism. Not only did that form of Sunni Islam become the official state religion, but ancestors of Muhammad ibn Abd al-Wahhab filled the ranks of the *ulema*, the Islamic scholars who advised the king.

Today, nearly 90 years after its founding, Saudi Arabia remains an absolute monarchy, with the king ruling by decree. For this reason, some people have suggested that Saudi Arabia isn't a true theocracy. But this begs the question. In Saudi Arabia, all citizens must be Muslims, and the practice of any religion other than Islam is prohibited. Civil law mirrors the ultraconservative Wahhabi interpretation of Sharia, which everyone is bound to follow. Religious police commonly known as *mutaween*—officially, the Committee for the Protection of Virtue and the Suppression of Vice—patrol public spaces and mete out punishment for Sharia offenses. These offenses include being in the company of a person of the opposite sex who isn't a close relative; the use of alcohol; immodest dress; and, for women, driving a car.

The *mutaween* drew international attention—and provoked outrage—in 2002. In March of that year, a girls' school in Mecca caught fire. But when the students tried to flee, they were blocked by members of the Committee for the Protection of Virtue and the Suppression of Vice. The reason? The schoolgirls weren't wearing the long robes and headscarves required of women in public. At least 14 students died as a result.

Iran

Like Saudi Arabia, Iran has large reserves of oil. That fact has played a major role in the modern history of the country.

Iran, called Persia until 1935, has a long and rich history. It has given birth to several major empires, beginning with the Achaemenid dynasty in the sixth century BCE, and it has been conquered and incorporated into other empires. For centuries, Zoroastrianism was Iran's dominant religion. In 636 CE, however, Arab conquerors overthrew the Persian Sassanid dynasty and brought Islam. Shia became the official form of Islam in the early 1500s, with the establishment of the Safavid dynasty. (Today about 9 in 10 Iranians are Shia Muslims.)

Iran's rulers wielded absolute authority until the 20th century. In 1906 widespread unrest forced the shah, or king, to accept the establishment of a parliament, called the Majlis. The shah also agreed to a constitution limiting his powers. In spite of these concessions, the shah did his best to thwart the Majlis. For years the legislature struggled with the king for power.

In 1908 a British group discovered oil in Iran and formed the Anglo-Persian Oil Company (APOC). The terms of APOC's agreement with Iran were highly favorable to the British company: Iran received royalties of just 16 percent on APOC's net profits. Many Iranians bristled at this arrangement, which they viewed as foreign exploitation.

In 1921 an Iranian army officer named Reza Khan staged a *coup*. Within five years, he had himself crowned shah, ruling as Reza Shah Pahlavi. He undertook a program to modernize Iran's economy.

Reza Shah declared Iran neutral during World War II.

Concerned about the security of Iran's oilfields, British authorities asked the shah to expel all German citizens from his country. He refused, and in 1941 British and Soviet forces invaded Iran and deposed the shah. His son, Mohammad Reza Pahlavi, was installed on the throne.

In 1951 Mohammad Mossadeq, Iran's prime minister, convinced the Majlis to vote to nationalize the oil industry. British interests—particularly the Anglo-Iranian Oil Company, as APOC had been renamed—stood to lose out. Great Britain imposed a blockade, preventing Iran from exporting any oil. The toll on the Iranian economy was considerable.

The shah sided with the British in the oil dispute. By August 1953 widespread dissatisfaction with his rule forced the shah to flee the country. That exile wouldn't last long, however. With assistance from the British intelligence service, the U.S. Central Intelligence Agency organized a coup that removed Prime Minister Mossadeq and returned the shah to power.

In the years that followed, the shah tightened his grip on Iran. With American assistance, he set up a secret police organization known as the SAVAK. It spied on Iranian citizens and arrested, tortured, and in many cases executed people who expressed opposition to the shah's rule.

The brutality of the SAVAK was one reason many Iranians turned against the shah. But it was by no means the only reason. The shah and the rest of the royal family had a well-earned reputation for taking much of Iran's wealth for themselves. The shah's campaign to modernize and Westernize Iran— called the White Revolution—was also highly unpopular.

Land-reform measures angered Iran's landowning elite while failing to improve the lives of peasants, many of whom migrated to cities. The traditional merchant class, known as *bazaari*, also felt threatened by the White Revolution's economic reforms. Conservative Muslims objected to political and social reforms aimed at improving the status of women. These included giving women the right to vote, compulsory education of girls as well as boys, and the adoption of Western fashions.

By the late 1970s, opposition to the shah's regime was broad based. But that opposition coalesced around a single Muslim *cleric*: Ruhollah Khomeini. An early critic of the White Revolution, Khomeini—an ayatollah, or high-ranking Shia scholar—had been jailed and then sent into exile in 1964. He continued to write and speak against the shah from Iraq and, later, France. He said that Iran must rid itself of corrupt foreigners and Western influences and return to its Islamic roots. Inside Iran, Khomeini won support from Shia *mullahs* (educated religious leaders). His sermons, smuggled into Iran from abroad, were read in many of Iran's mosques during Friday prayers.

The Islamic Revolution

Mass demonstrations, riots, and strikes broke out across Iran in 1978. The shah declared martial law and attempted to put down the unrest by force, but this backfired. The number of protesters only grew. In early January 1979, the shah appointed a liberal opposition leader, Shapour Bakhtiar, as prime minister. Yet this, too, failed to placate the regime's critics. On January 16, the shah left Iran.

Two weeks later, on February 1, Ayatollah Khomeini made a triumphant return to Iran. Millions of people crowded into the streets of Tehran, the capital, to greet him. Khomeini immediately made it clear that he had no intention of working with Bakhtiar, who had promised to bring democracy to Iran. Khomeini named his own interim prime minister, declaring that it was the religious duty of all Shia in the country to follow him.

Fighting soon erupted between followers of Khomeini and forces that remained loyal to Bakhtiar's government. On February 11, after military units began defecting to the side of the revolutionaries, Iran's top military leaders declared that the armed forces would remain neutral in the unfolding political conflict. That essentially marked the end of Bakhtiar's government.

The Ayatollah Ruhollah Khomeini (1902–1989) was an architect of the 1979 revolution in Iran that removed the American-supported ruler, Shah Mohammad Reza Pahlavi, from power. Once Khomeini and his followers gained control of Iran, they established a government in which Shiite religious leaders held both political and religious authority.

The dizzying collapse of the old regime left a power vacuum. Local Islamic councils arose to fill the void, but in much of the country there was virtually no functioning civil authority. In this chaotic environment, a nationwide referendum was hastily held, on March 30 and 31. Iranians voted to approve an Islamic repub-

The current flag of Iran, adopted after the 1979 revolution, reflects the country's status as a theocracy. The red symbol in the center is a version of the Islamic statement of belief: "There is no god but Allah," while the writing on the green and red bands, in the script used for the Quran, reads, "Allah is great."

lic. On April 1, 1979, Ayatollah Khomeini officially proclaimed the founding of the Islamic Republic of Iran.

Many Iranians had yet to appreciate fully what that meant. Khomeini may have been the face of the Iranian revolution, the individual around whom the shah's opponents had rallied. But the anti-shah coalition as a whole didn't necessarily share his vision for a future Iranian government. In fact, few people knew precisely what his vision for a future government was. Most Iranians assumed that Khomeini would act merely as a spiritual guide for their country. However, he intended to create an Islamic theocracy—with himself at the head.

Former allies in the movement to topple the shah found themselves pushed aside by Khomeini's religious followers. There would be no broad-based coalition in the new Iranian government. Government posts were steadily filled with Muslim clerics loyal to the ayatollah. Those who objected were often subject to violence.

In late April 1979, Khomeini ordered an assembly to convene to draft a new constitution. His instructions were clear. "You are here to create a Constitution that is 100 percent Islamic," the ayatollah declared. "Not a single clause, not a single phrase can be devoid of the Islamic spirit."

The delegates did as they were told. The constitution they drafted, which went into effect at the end of 1979, guaranteed that the power of Iran's Shia clerics would be virtually unchallengeable, despite a veneer of democracy.

The constitution created the position of Supreme Leader—with Khomeini the first person to fill the role. The Supreme Leader is Iran's head of state as well as its top-ranking Islamic cleric. He serves for life. The Supreme Leader appoints (directly or indirectly) the members of a committee of Islamic legal authorities known as the Council of Guardians. Under Iran's constitution, this 12-member group has the authority to reject as un-Islamic any law passed by the Iranian parliament. Iranian citizens do vote for members of parliament and for president. However, the Iranian constitution requires all would-be candidates to receive the approval of the Council of Guardians. This gives the clerical establishment another powerful tool for preventing challenges to their authority. In 2009, for example, the Council of Guardians rejected nearly 500 presidential aspirants, permitting just four candidates on the ballot.

An Uncompromising Theocracy

As Supreme Leader, Ayatollah Khomeini set about reshaping Iranian society. He systematically eliminated the Western cultural influences that had taken hold under the shah. Sharia was introduced, with much stricter limits on women's freedom. Morality police rooted out Sharia violations. Penalties were often harsh.

In the realm of foreign policy, Khomeini charted a confrontational course. He consistently referred to the United States as "the Great Satan," and in November 1979, when militant Iranian students seized the U.S. Embassy in Tehran and took its staff hostage, his government refused to intervene. The American hostages were freed only after 444 days of captivity.

Khomeini actively sought to export the Islamic revolution abroad. In neighboring Iraq, he fomented opposition to the secular regime of dictator Saddam Hussein. In 1980 Saddam ordered an invasion of Iran, and a brutal but inconclusive eight-year war ensued.

Khomeini died in 1989. His successor, Ayatollah Ali Khamenei, has in some respects promoted an even stricter interpretation of Sharia. Under Khamenei, Iran's foreign policy has remained bellicose. Iran is widely believed to sponsor terrorist organizations, and on several occasions its leaders have threatened to annihilate Israel. Iran's nuclear program, which most independent analysts say is directed toward the development of nuclear weapons, has triggered a variety of international sanctions. Iran's economy has struggled in recent years as a result of those sanctions.

Iran is a closed society. But there are indications of considerable dissatisfaction with the regime. For example, in December 2017 and January 2018, Iranians protested against the theocratic regime and its economic policies. Protests and anti-government demonstrations occurred in more than 70

Iranian cities. In the end, the Iranian police cracked down on protesters, killing several dozen and arresting thousands

Afghanistan: Land of Perpetual Conflict

Afghanistan, which borders Iran to the east, also produced a modern Islamic theocracy. But in most other respects, Afghanistan couldn't be more different from its Persian neighbor. Afghanistan lacks valuable mineral resources. It is very poor. It has almost no history of strong centralized government; loyalty to tribe remains of primary importance. About 80 percent of Afghanistan's people follow the Sunni branch of Islam.

Afghanistan has seen its share of invading armies throughout history. The extremely rugged terrain and fiercely independent tribal people have in almost every case brought grief upon would-be conquerors. For much of the 19th century, the British tried to conquer Afghanistan to prevent the expanding Russian Empire from cutting off Britain's India colony. In 1880, after two costly wars, the British abandoned the effort and settled for a treaty that allowed Great Britain to exercise control over Afghanistan's foreign policy.

In 1919, however, Emir Amanullah Khan repudiated that agreement and declared Afghanistan's independence from all British influence. But Amanullah's introduction of social reforms angered tribal leaders, who forced him to flee the country in 1929. Several years of bloody conflict followed before Mohammad Zahir Shah emerged as king in 1933. He ruled for four decades, until he was overthrown in a 1973 coup led by his cousin, General Mohammad Daoud Khan.

Daoud served as president until 1978, when he was assassinated. Communists seized power, but they were highly unpopular.

In December 1979, Soviet troops invaded Afghanistan. Their mission was supposed to be straightforward: to prop up Afghanistan's Communist government. But what ensued was a brutal, decade-long war. While Soviet forces controlled Afghanistan's cities, they weren't able to defeat Afghan guerrilla fighters known as *mujahideen* in the rugged countryside. The mujahideen—Muslim "holy warriors"—received weapons and money from various countries, including the United States and Saudi Arabia.

During the war, several million Afghanis fled the country. Many ended up in Pakistan. These refugees were never integrated into Pakistani society. To provide for the education of some of the refugee children, Saudi Arabia sponsored all-male religious schools known as madrassas. In these schools, Afghan boys were exposed to several strains of conservative Islam, including Wahhabism and Deobandi, an Islamic movement that originated in India and that calls for a rejection of Western influences.

The Rise and Fall of the Taliban

In 1989 Soviet troops finally pulled out of Afghanistan. Unfortunately, this didn't bring peace. The mujahideen continued fighting to topple Afghanistan's Communist government. They succeeded in 1992, but after that a bloody civil war broke out as mujahideen groups battled one another for control. Afghanistan was plunged into chaos. Former mujahideen leaders ruled parts of the country as warlords. They were corrupt and brutal.

In 1994, in Afghanistan's southern province of Kandahar, a small group of fighters seized and executed a warlord who had committed an especially heinous act. The group, led by a former mujahideen named Mullah Mohammed Omar, called itself the Taliban.

 Ancient Writing

Taliban means "students" in Pashto, one of Afghanistan's main languages. As refugees during the Soviet occupation, many of Mullah Omar's followers were students at Saudi-sponsored madrassas in Pakistan.

The Taliban appealed to many Afghanis by promising to bring order. The group's numbers swelled. After taking Kandahar Province in 1994, the Taliban set out to conquer all of Afghanistan. By September 1996, when the capital city of Kabul fell, most (though not all) of the country was under Taliban control.

Mullah Omar was declared *Amir ul-Momineen*, or Commander of the Faithful. The government was an absolute theocracy, with power concentrated in his hands. All government decisions would be "based on the advice of the Amir ul-Momineen," explained a Taliban spokesman.

> For us consultation is not necessary. We believe that this is in line with the Sharia. We abide by the Amir's view even if he alone takes this view. There will not be a head of state. . . . Mullah Omar will be the highest authority and the government will not be able to implement any decision to which he does not agree.

Under Mullah Omar, the Taliban imposed an ultra-strict version of Sharia. Women faced especially harsh restrictions.

They were forbidden to hold jobs. They weren't permitted to go out in public unless accompanied by a male relative. When they did go out, women had to be covered from head to toe in a burqa and were prohibited from talking to unrelated males. Even laughing loudly was forbidden, as the Taliban believed that no stranger should ever hear a woman's voice. Because male doctors generally weren't allowed to see female patients, and because with few exceptions female doctors weren't allowed to practice medicine at all, thousands of women died in childbirth or from treatable illnesses.

Men had to grow beards longer than a fist. They had to wear loose-fitting robes and caps. Attendance at a mosque for daily prayers was mandatory. No one was allowed to listen to music on records, tapes, or the radio. TV, movies, and the Internet were banned. Games and pastimes such as chess, dancing, and kite flying were outlawed.

Afghanis who violated the Taliban's Sharia rules faced harsh punishment. Women whose burqas didn't cover their ankles, for example, were whipped by the Taliban's morality police. Men whose beards weren't long enough were beaten. Women who were discovered wearing nail polish had their fingers cut off. Women accused of inappropriate contact with men were stoned to death.

The Taliban's policies outraged the international community. Only three countries—Saudi Arabia, Pakistan, and the United Arab Emirates—recognized the Taliban as Afghanistan's legitimate government. Ultimately, however, it was the Taliban's decision to provide sanctuary for Saudi-born terrorist leader Osama bin Laden that led to the regime's downfall.

Bin Laden—a financial supporter of the Taliban regime—had been living in Afghanistan for about five years when his al-Qaeda organization carried out the September 11, 2001, terrorist attacks against the United States. American officials demanded that the Taliban turn Bin Laden over to face punishment. The Taliban refused.

In October 2001, the United States and allied countries began a military campaign in Afghanistan. By year's end the Taliban had been routed, and Afghanistan's harsh theocracy was swept away. However, the group continued fighting against the U.S.-backed Afghan government. By 2018, it was estimated that the Taliban controlled about 10 percent of the country.

 Text-Dependent Questions

1. What is Sharia law?
2. What are the two major sects, or branches, of Islam?
3. What is the function of the *mutaween* in Saudi Arabia?
4. What religious leader inspired the 1979 Iranian Revolution?

 Research Project

Using your school library or the internet, find out more about the Prophet Muhammad. How did he establish the first Muslim state after leaving Mecca and traveling to Medina in 622 ce? Write a two-page biography and share it with your class.

Thousands of pilgrims gather outside St. Peter's Basilica in Vatican City, the world's smallest independent state. The Roman Catholic pope is the Vatican's political and spiritual leader.

 Words to Understand in This Chapter

excommunicate—to officially exclude from participation in the sacraments of the church.

pagan—a person who follows a polytheistic religion, or who believes in multiple gods.

polygamy—the practice of having more than one spouse at the same time; also called plural marriage.

treason—the crime of betraying one's country or trying to overthrow one's government.

4 Western Theocracies

I n the Gospel of Matthew, Jesus draws a distinction between secular and religious authority when he says, "Give to Caesar what is Caesar's, but give to God what is God's."

Christians haven't always been content to keep religion and the state separate, however. In Europe, Protestant leader John Calvin created a strict theocracy in the city of Geneva, Switzerland, during the 1550s. A century later in America, Puritans set up a theocracy in the Massachusetts colony. Mormon settlers did the same in Utah Territory during the late 1800s. All of these theocracies were relatively short lived. Theocracies headed by the popes of the Roman Catholic Church proved more enduring.

The Papal States

By the early Middle Ages, the Roman Catholic Church controlled significant tracts of land, much of it on the Italian peninsula. But while the pope claimed spiritual authority as leader of the Church, he didn't rule a sovereign state. He wasn't head of a civil government. That changed in the eighth century.

In the early 750s, the Catholic Church was in conflict with the Lombards, a mostly *pagan* tribe from Germany that had ruled a large part of Italy for 200 years. In 753 Pope Steven II made an alliance with Pepin the Short, leader of the Franks, a tribe that lived in what is now France. The pope officially recognized Pepin as "King of the Franks." In return, Pepin sent an army to Italy to fight the Lombards.

After Pepin defeated the Lombards, he made a gift to the Church of some of the conquered lands. This was known as the Donation of 754. Pepin specified that the pope was to govern the donated territory as both a civil and a spiritual leader. These lands were the first Papal States.

Eventually the Papal States would stretch in a diagonal band across Italy, from near Venice all the way to Rome. For more than 1,000 years, the Papal States were a theocracy. They were ruled by successive popes of the Roman Catholic Church.

During the 1800s, the various smaller states that existed on the Italian peninsula were unified into the Kingdom of Italy.

Key Idea

Theocratic governments enforce moral and religious values not only in civic affairs but also in their citizens' private lives.

The flag of Vatican City was adopted in 1929, when the Lateran Treaty was signed. The gold and silver keys on the flag represent the authority claimed by the Roman Catholic Church over both spiritual and worldly matters.

The process was completed in 1870, when Italian forces defeated the army of the Papal States and captured Rome. Pope Pius IX didn't officially acknowledge the loss of the Papal States, but the land was incorporated into the Kingdom of Italy. The pope continued to control a small parcel of territory atop Rome's Vatican Hill.

Vatican City State

During the 1920s, the Church officially gave up any claim to the former Papal States. The Lateran Treaty, signed in 1929,

In 2013, Pope Francis became the 266th head of the Roman Catholic Church and ruler of Vatican City.

compensated the Church for the loss of territory and established Vatican City as a sovereign state. This 100-acre realm, located within Rome, is an absolute theocracy led by the pope. Article 1 of the Fundamental Law of Vatican City State reads, "The Supreme Pontiff [the pope], Sovereign of Vatican City State, has the fullness of legislative, executive, and judicial powers." According to Roman Catholic doctrine, the pope answers only to God.

About 800 people live in Vatican City. Almost all are clergy or work for the Vatican. The Vatican has its own license plates, coins, postage stamps, and passports. When the pope travels to other countries, he is treated as a head of state, not a private citizen, and he has Permanent Observer status at the United Nations.

The Geneva Theocracy

In 1517 Martin Luther, a Catholic monk, wrote a list of objections to certain practices of the Catholic Church that he considered wrong. Luther didn't want to break away from the

Church—he simply wanted to reform it. Nevertheless, the pope *excommunicated* him. But this didn't stop Luther from promoting his ideas, which spread across Europe and gave rise to a separate branch of Christianity known as Protestantism. The movement by which this occurred is called the Reformation.

John Calvin, born in France in 1509 and educated as a lawyer, broke with the Catholic Church in 1530. From then on, he devoted himself to the ideals of the Reformation. In 1535 Calvin moved to Geneva, Switzerland. There he established a church, enforced a strict code of behavior, and began to reorganize the city council.

 Calvinist Beliefs

John Calvin preached the following beliefs in the Reformed church he established in Geneva. These ideas influenced many reformers who followed him.

- God is superior to all governments and rules the world with total and absolute authority.

- A literal interpretation of the Bible is all that is needed for organizing the church, the government, and private life.

- Anything not specifically mentioned in the Bible should be rejected; anything mentioned should be followed exactly without any room for interpretation.

- God chooses or preordains who will be saved at birth. Calvin called these people "living saints" or "visible saints." No one else can be saved, even by doing good works or living a pious life. People who behave immorally show that they are not visible saints.

The religious reformer John Calvin (1509–1564) was the spiritual leader of the community in Geneva, a city in Europe that is now part of Switzerland. During the 16th century Geneva became an important center of Protestant Christianity. This monument in Geneva includes statues of important Reformation leaders, including Calvin, William Farel, Theodore Beza, and John Knox.

Resistance to his ideas forced Calvin to leave Geneva for several years. When he returned, he formed a joint church-civil court called the Consistory. It disciplined people for violating church and moral rules. Twelve Elders chosen by the court became morality police responsible for monitoring citizens' behavior.

"It was as if the doors of the houses had suddenly been thrown open and as if the walls had been transformed into glass," one writer noted.

> From moment to moment, by day and by night, there might come a knocking at the entry, and a number of the "spiritual police" announce a "visitation" without the concerned citizen's being able to offer resistance. Once a month rich and poor, the powerful and the weak, had to submit to the questioning of these [morality police]. . . . For hours . . . hitherto trusted men must be examined like schoolboys as to whether they knew the prayers by heart, or as to why they had failed to attend one of Master Calvin's sermons. . . . They felt the women's dresses to see whether their skirts were not too long or too short, whether these garments had superfluous frills or dangerous slits. The police . . . counted the rings on the victim's fingers, and looked to see how many pairs of shoes there were in the cupboard.

At first, there was some opposition to the morality police, but by 1555 John Calvin had almost uncontested power. He expanded the enforcement authority of the Consistory. Members of Calvin's Reformed church who were persecuted in other countries because of their beliefs began arriving in Geneva. This gave Calvin an expanded base of support. All who disagreed with him were punished.

After Calvin's death in 1564, religious control gradually loosened, and Geneva no longer functioned as a theocracy. Many foreign Reformed believers left the city and carried

Calvin's ideas back to their home countries and, eventually, to America.

The Puritan Theocracy in Massachusetts

The Puritans were an English Protestant group founded around 1560. They wanted to "purify" the Church of England, or Anglican Church. By the early 1600s, the Puritans—whose beliefs were almost identical to those of John Calvin and his followers—faced an increasingly hostile religious and political environment in England. In 1630 about 1,000 Puritans under the leadership of John Winthrop sailed to America. They followed a smaller group of Puritans who had crossed the Atlantic Ocean the previous year. The Puritans settled near present-day Boston and founded the Massachusetts Bay Colony.

Like Calvin, the Puritans believed civil government should follow the laws of God to ensure the spiritual welfare of the community. Also like Calvin, they believed in the doctrine of visible saints. Only visible saints—those people who could show by their behavior and testimony that God had chosen them to be saved—were allowed to be church members. The policy of excluding the "ungodly" was their way of strengthening religion in the community and making the government operate in the interest of their beliefs.

The Massachusetts Bay Colony was different from most other theocracies in that it had elected leaders (only free, male church members were allowed to vote) rather than a single tyrant who dictated and enforced the law. But like other theocracies it punished any deviation in belief or acceptable behavior.

Beginning in 1629 and 1630, thousands of men, women, and children made the two-month voyage from England to North America. They wanted to escape persecution and to manage their new community, the Massachusetts Bay Colony, according to their religious beliefs.

Religious Rejection

The Puritans excluded anyone from their community who did not wholly accept their beliefs. In 1635 Roger Williams, a Puritan minister, was tried in court for having dangerous ideas. His crime was to advocate the separation of church and state. Williams was found guilty and banished from Massachusetts. He went on to found Rhode Island, the first American colony to guarantee freedom of worship to followers of all religions.

The Puritan theocracy began to break down after the first generation of immigrants died. The infamous Salem witch trials of 1692–93 further eroded the power of the theocracy. Nevertheless, Puritan beliefs influenced the laws of Massachusetts for many years.

The Founding of the Latter-day Saints

One other American theocracy arose from a new religion—the Church of Jesus Christ of Latter-day Saints, commonly called the LDS or Mormon Church. Between 1820 and 1827 a young man living in upstate New York, Joseph Smith, claimed to have had three visions. In the last, an angel named Moroni directed Smith to a hill near Palmyra, New York, and instructed him to dig up golden plates that had been buried there some 1,400 years earlier. The plates, Smith said, were engraved with a sort of hieroglyphic writing. Smith was able to decipher it with the help of special eyeglasses provided by the angel. Translated, the text on the golden plates became the Book of Mormon—sacred scripture as well as an account of the ancient inhabitants of

America. It would form the basis of LDS beliefs and—in the view of Mormons—confirm Joseph Smith's status as a prophet.

By 1830 Smith had a small group of followers in western New York state. Encountering some hostility, Smith and the Mormons moved to Kirtland, Ohio, and later to Independence, Missouri. All the while, Smith claimed to receive many revelations from God. In Missouri, violent clashes erupted between the growing Mormon community and non-Mormons. Once again, Smith moved his followers, this time to Nauvoo, Illinois. There the Mormon community grew rapidly.

In Nauvoo, Smith reported a revelation that God wanted the

Although Joseph Smith (1805–1844) established the Mormon religion in New York, he and his followers eventually left the state, settling first in northern Ohio and later in Missouri and Illinois.

Mormons to practice *polygamy*, or plural marriage. This proved especially controversial, helping to create a rift within the Mormon community.

In 1844 dissenting Mormons in Nauvoo founded a rival church. They published a newspaper that included articles criticizing Smith for his polygamy and accusing him of wanting to establish a large-scale theocracy, with himself as king. Smith responded by ordering armed followers to destroy the rival church's printing press. That provoked his arrest by local authorities. Smith was charged with inciting a riot and, later, with committing *treason* against the state of Illinois. Smith was in jail in the town of Carthage, awaiting trial, when a mob killed him on June 27, 1844.

The Kingdom of God in Utah Territory

In 1846 Brigham Young, one of Smith's trusted advisers, led most of Nauvoo's Mormons west. Many would settle around Utah's Great Salt Lake.

The Mormon community at Nauvoo had been a theocracy, ruled by Joseph Smith and administered by a dozen of his apostles known as the Quorum of Twelve. In Utah, Brigham Young expanded theocratic rule. The Mormons, he said, were establishing the Kingdom of God on Earth, in preparation for the Second Coming of Jesus.

 Educational Video

To learn more about how the Mormons moved West to Utah, scan here:

Led by Brigham Young, thousands of Mormon pioneers set out from Nauvoo, Illinois, across the Great Plains in 1846. They settled in present-day Utah, establishing Salt Lake City and other communities.

Joseph Smith had outlined the idea of "theodemocracy"—a blend of democratic practices with theocracy. Smith envisioned a government by God and righteous men.

Brigham Young claimed to pursue the goal of theodemocracy. On the surface at least, the Mormon community under his leadership did include democratic elections. However, votes weren't secret. No one Young didn't support was ever elected, and only laws he approved of were passed.

In 1849 Young petitioned the U.S. government to admit to the Union the Mormon "State of Deseret." This huge new state

Brigham Young (1801–1877) took over leadership of the Church of Jesus Christ of Latter-day Saints after Joseph Smith's death. Young led the Mormons west to Mexican territory that is now the state of Utah.

would cover much of the territory the United States had gained as a result of the Mexican War, including most of present-day Utah, Nevada, and Arizona, along with parts of California, New Mexico, Colorado, Idaho, and Wyoming. The U.S. Congress balked, instead organizing the smaller Utah Territory in 1850. Young was appointed its governor.

Tensions between the federal government and the government of Utah Territory soon bubbled up. As non-Mormon settlers entered the territory, bloody clashes with Mormons erupted. Brigham Young was accused of failing to enforce federal law, and instead ruling Utah Territory as a personal theocracy. In 1857 President James Buchanan sent U.S. troops to Utah to impose federal authority. Brigham Young was replaced as governor the following year. After the outbreak of the Civil War in 1861, U.S. troops were withdrawn, and the Mormon theocracy once again gained practical, if not legal, control of the Utah Territory.

Brigham Young wanted Utah to become part of the United States, but only on his terms. In 1856 he wrote, "As the Lord lives, we are bound to become a sovereign state in the Union or an independent nation by ourselves." Utah Territory was repeatedly rejected for statehood because of its acceptance of polygamy and the absence of secret ballots in elections. Finally, in 1890 Wilford Woodruff, who had become LDS president after Young's death in 1877, issued a public statement rejecting polygamy. This and other concessions paved the way for Utah's admission into the Union. In 1896, when Utah became the 45th state, the vestiges of the Mormon theocracy that had once flourished were erased forever.

 Text-Dependent Questions

1. Who made the Donation of 754 to the Roman Catholic Church?
2. What was the result of the Lateran Treaty, signed in 1929?
3. In what Swiss city did John Calvin establish a theocracy during the sixteenth century?

 Research Project

Using your school library or the internet, find out more about the Protestant Reformation of the sixteenth and seventeenth centuries. How did the Reformation challenge the authority of the Roman Catholic Church in Europe? How did the Roman Catholic Church's response to the Reformation? Write a two-page paper and present it to your class.

The flag of the Islamic State of Iraq and the Levant (ISIL), a group of Islamic fundamentalists who established a theocratic government over territory they controlled in the Middle East from 2013 to 2017.

 Words to Understand in This Chapter

drone strike—an attack in which an unmanned aerial vehicle fires missiles or explosives at a target on the ground, such as a building, vehicle, or enemy commander.

Enlightenment—a philosophical movement of the 17th and 18th centuries. The Enlightenment was characterized by belief in the power of human reason, which led to major changes in political, religious, and educational doctrine.

5 The Future of Theocracies

The essence of theocracy is the imposition of one group's religious views on all members of society. Theocracies, by their very nature, limit the freedom of individuals. They punish failure to conform in matters of belief and in matters of personal moral behavior.

Theocracy is incompatible with the Western liberal tradition that grew out of the European *Enlightenment*, a wide-ranging philosophical movement of the 17th and 18th centuries. Enlightenment thinkers asserted the importance of personal liberty. They said that individuals should be able to live their lives as they saw fit (provided they didn't harm other people). Governments had no business telling their citizens what to believe. Everyone should be free to follow the religion of his or her choosing—or not to follow any religion at all.

Today freedom of religion is accepted as a foundation of all liberal societies. In many Western countries, it is explicitly written into law. In the United States, for example, the First Amendment to the Constitution guarantees that the government won't infringe on citizens' religious freedom.

Obstacles to Theocracy

The United States—a nation of immigrants—has long been a very diverse society. Americans come from a multitude of ethnic and cultural backgrounds. They've inherited a variety of faith traditions from their forebears. Increasingly, other countries around the world are becoming similarly diverse.

Diversity of beliefs makes a theocracy much less likely to arise—or, if it already exists, much more difficult to sustain. Theocratic governments tend to be stable only when a large proportion of the people follow the dominant religion.

But even where an overwhelming majority of the population shares the same faith, theocracy won't necessarily be popular. In Iran, for instance, 98 percent of the people are Muslims. Yet in a recent survey by the Gallup World Poll, only 13 percent of Iranians said that Sharia should be the sole basis for legislation.

In the rare cases that a theocracy has arisen in recent times, it has always been in a country torn by war, political turmoil, or social upheaval. Chaotic conditions may make "rule by God" seem like an appealing option—as was the case in Afghanistan when the Taliban first emerged. Alternatively, such conditions may give potential theocrats space to maneuver their way into power—as, arguably, was the case in Iran during the Islamic

A guard looks at Syrian refugees in a camp on the Turkey-Syria border. Destabilizing events like civil wars and famines can create conditions in which a theocratic regime can attempt to seize power, as has occurred recently in places like Syria and Somalia.

Revolution, as well as in Syria and Iraq during 2013 and 2014, when a group known as the Islamic State gained control over large areas of territory.

Rise and Fall of the Islamic State

During late 2010 and early 2011, anti-government protests began to occur in a number of Arab countries. The protests—which became known as the "Arab Spring"—were aimed at improving the political circumstances and living conditions of the Arab people. In Syria, demonstrations in the city of Daraa criticized the authoritarian regime of Syrian dictator Bashar al-Assad. The Syrian government responded by arresting the students who were responsible, leading to more protests. The unrest soon spread throughout the country.

By August 2011, the protests had turned into a violent uprising against the Assad government. The United Nations and many countries condemned the Syrian government's use of heavy weapons against rebel forces, as well as the killing of civilians. Several countries, including the United States and Turkey, began to arm and train rebel groups, while militant Islamist groups in places like Iraq and Libya began to send fighters to Syria.

During 2013 and 2014, an Islamist group that called itself the Islamic State of Iraq and the Levant (ISIL) was able to gain control of territory in both Iraq and Syria. In June 2014, after conquering the Iraqi city of Mosul, ISIL declared itself to be the restoration of the Islamic caliphate. ISIL's extremist leaders claimed that all Muslims needed to swear allegiance to their theocracy and follow its dictates, and that Islam needed to be returned to a "pure" state by eliminating apostates, or those who do not follow their teachings. ISIL attempted to do this in the territories it controlled by murdering Christians, Jews, Kurds, Shiite Muslims, Druze, and others living in the regions it controlled. These atrocities led to military intervention in the Syrian civil war by the United States, Russia, Turkey, France, and other countries. Airstrikes were launched against ISIL positions, although the U.S. and other countries decided not to send in soldiers to wage ground combat.

One of ISIL's stated goals was to bring about a clash with the non-Muslim world, which (according to its leader's beliefs) the Muslims were destined to win. ISIL's murders of Christians and westerners were devoted to this end. The organization attacked religious sites in Syria and Iraq, including Shiite mosques and Christian churches. ISIL also destroyed ancient historical sites, including a pagan temple and a Roman theater in Palmyra, Syria, and structures built during the Assyrian period in Iraq that date back more than 2,500 years.

ISIL also attempted to attack the West directly, in hopes of inciting an invasion by ground troops in response. In 2015 and 2016, members of the group carried out terrorist attacks in many countries, including Belgium, France, Great Britain, Iran, Russia, Tunisia, and Turkey.

By the end of 2015, approximately 5 million people in Iraq and Syria lived under the control of the ISIL theocracy. The group controlled oil-rich provinces of Iraq, which provided funds to support their conquests. However, the coordinated international military efforts against ISIL gradually chipped away at its strength. ISIL-held cities were gradually recaptured,

including Mosul, Iraq, in July 2017 and Raqqa, Syria, in
October of that year. By early 2018, ISIL only controlled a few
scattered communities in the deserts of Iraq and Syria.

Other Failed Theocracies

In any event, circumstances similar to those that gave rise to
theocracies in Iran, Afghanistan, and Syria have occurred in
other places. And on occasion they have led to attempts to
establish theocratic regimes. Somalia, a country located at the
Horn of Africa, is one example. In 1991 Somalia's central government collapsed. In 2006, after 15 years of fighting between
rival militia armies, a group called the Islamic Courts Union
(ICU) established a theocracy in the southern part of Somalia.
Although virtually everyone in Somalia is a Sunni Muslim, the
ICU theocracy lasted less than a year. Beginning in 2009,
another militant Islamic group, known as Al-Shabaab, imposed
Sharia in the parts of Somalia it controlled. By 2012, though,
Al-Shabaab had suffered a series of crushing defeats at the

hands of African Union forces and troops loyal to Somalia's transitional government. In 2014, Al-Shabaab leader Ahmed Abdi Godane was killed in a drone strike by the U.S. military. However, the group has continued to carry out terrorist attacks in Somalia in hopes of achieving its goals.

The failure of theocracy to take root in Somalia—where conditions would seem highly favorable to this form of government—hints at just how difficult establishing theocratic rule over a nation actually is. Still, the possibility that a theocratic regime may come to power in some other majority-Muslim country cannot be discounted. But it is highly unlikely that theocracy will spread very far. In the modern world, theocratic governance seems increasingly outdated.

 Text-Dependent Questions

1. Why is theocracy incompatible with the Western liberal tradition?
2. What was the Arab Spring?

 Research Project

Read or watch contemporary news reports about the Islamic State of Iraq and the Levant (ISIL). What were some of the the goals of this theocratic organization's leaders? Were they able to achieve those goals? Why or why not? Write a two-page report and share it with your class, using examples to support your conclusions.

Series Glossary of Key Terms

autonomy—the right of self-government.

aristocracy—an elite or upper class of society whose members hold hereditary titles or offices; a ruling class or nobility.

BCE **and** CE—an alternative to the traditional Western designation of calendar eras, which used the birth of Jesus as a dividing line. BCE stands for "Before the Common Era," and is equivalent to BC ("Before Christ"). Dates labeled CE, or "Common Era," are equivalent to *Anno Domini* (AD, or "the Year of Our Lord").

civil society—the sum total of institutions, organizations, and groups promoting social and civic causes in a country (for example, human rights groups, labor unions, arts foundations) that are not funded or controlled by the government or business interests.

colonialism—control or domination by one country over an area or people outside its boundaries; the policy of colonizing foreign lands.

communism—a system in which property and goods are owned or controlled by the state.

democracy—a system of government in which political authority is retained by the people, who exercise this authority through voting.

ideology—a system of beliefs, values, and ideas forming the basis of a social, economic, or political philosophy.

monarchy—a system of government in which a monarch reigns over a state or territory, usually for life and by hereditary right.

nationalism—the belief that shared ethnicity, language, and history should form the basis for political organization; the desire of people with a common culture to have their own state.

oligarchy—a form of government in which a small group of people holds power, often for their own benefit.

plutocracy—a form of government in which the very wealthy rule.

self-determination—determination by a people of their own future political status.

theocracy—a system of government in which religious leaders rule in the name of God or a deity.

totalitarianism—an extreme form of authoritarianism in which the state seeks to control all aspects of citizens' lives.

Chronology

ca. 3100 BCE: Egypt is united under one ruler who is considered a god. This is the first known example of a theocracy.

ca. 2000 BCE: The Maya establish city-states, each ruled by a god-king.

ca. 250–900 CE: The Mayan civilization reaches its peak.

610: Muhammad ibn Abdullah, the Prophet of Islam, says he receives the first of many revelations from God.

1521: The Spanish conquistador Hernán Cortés defeats the Aztecs.

1532: The Spanish conquistador Francisco Pizarro seizes the Inca emperor Atahuallpa and routs his army.

1535: John Calvin moves to Geneva, Switzerland, where he later establishes a Protestant theocracy.

1629–30: Puritans arrive in Massachusetts, where they establish a theocracy.

1827:	Joseph Smith claims to dig up golden plates on which are inscribed, in hieroglyphic writing, the Book of Mormon.
1844:	Joseph Smith is killed in Carthage, Illinois.
1847:	On July 21, Mormon settlers led by Brigham Young arrive in the Great Salt Lake valley.
1979:	Mohammad Reza Pahlavi, the shah of Iran, is overthrown; under the leadership of Ayatollah Ruhollah Khomeini, an Islamic theocracy is set up in Iran.
1996:	The Taliban capture Afghanistan's capital, Kabul, and proclaim Mullah Mohammad Omar Commander of the Faithful and leader of the government.
2001:	U.S. and allied forces attack Afghanistan and overthrow the Taliban regime in response to the September 11 terrorist attack.
2012:	Al-Shabaab, an Islamist militant group in Somalia, suffers defeats at the hands of African Union forces and troops loyal to Somalia's provisional government.
2014:	The Islamic State of Iraq and the Levant (ISIL) gains control of Mosul, Iraq, and declares the restoration of the caliphate.
2017	Kurdish and Syrian forces backed by the United States recapture territory from ISIL.
2018	Anti-government protests in Iran.

Further Reading

Ashkar, Michael. *Islam*. Philadelphia: Mason Crest, 2018.

Berlatsky, Noah, ed. *The Taliban*. Detroit: Greenhaven Press, 2011.

Bowen, Aaron. *Christianity*. Philadelphia: Mason Crest, 2018.

Goldstein, Natalie. *Religion and the State*. New York: Facts on File, 2010.

Sekulow, Jay. *Rise of ISIS: A Threat We Can't Ignore*. New York: Howard Books, 2014.

Shelley, Fred M. *Governments from Around the World: From Democracies to Theocracies*. Santa Barbara, Calif.: ABC-CLIO, 2016.

Stern, Jessica, and J.M. Berger. *ISIS: The State of Terror*. New York: Ecco, 2015.

Internet Resources

http://www.newadvent.org/cathen

This Internet version of the Catholic Encyclopedia provides articles on a variety of subjects related to the Roman Catholic Church.

http://www.pbs.org/empires/islam/

The companion website for the PBS documentary film *Islam: Empire of Faith* contains a wealth of information about the history of Islam.

http://www.pbs.org/mormons/

An introduction to the Church of Jesus Christ of Latter-day Saints, from the PBS series *American Experience*.

http://www.bbc.com/news/world-middle-east-29052144

The British Broadcasting Company (BBC) provides an overview of the Islamic State, with many useful graphics and videos.

Chapter Notes

p. 8–11:   "Some legislators have permitted . . ." Flavius Josephus, *The New Complete Works of Josephus*, translated by William Whiston (Grand Rapids, MI: Kregel Publications, 1999), 970.

p. 15:   "Theocratic, or to make . . ." Avihu Zakai, *Exile and Kingdom: History and Apocalypse in the Puritan Migration to America* (Cambridge, UK: Cambridge University Press, 2002), 235.

p. 40:   "The Medinan community . . ." John L. Esposito, *Islam: The Straight Path* (New York and Oxford, UK: Oxford University Press, 1988), 37.

p. 42:   "Give to Caesar . . ." Gospel of Matthew 23:21.

p. 42:   "In contrast to the belief . . ." John L. Esposito and Dalia Mogahed, *Who Speaks for Islam?* (New York: Gallup Press, 2007), 26–27.

p. 53:   "You are here to create . . ." Saul S. Friedman, *A History of the Middle East* (Jefferson, NC: McFarland & Co., 2006), 292.

p. 57:   "based on the advice . . ." Ahmed Rashid, *Taliban: Militant Islam, Oil and Fundamentalism in Central Asia*, 2nd ed. (New Haven, CT: Yale University Press, 2010), 102.

p. 64: "The Supreme Pontiff . . ." Vatican Information Service, "Vatican City State Has a New Constitution," February 1, 2001. http://visnews-en.blogspot.com/2001/02/vatican-city-state-has-new-constitution.html

p. 67: "It was as if . . ." Ronald Wintrobe and Fabio Padovano, "Spiritual Monopoly and Dictatorship." In Mario Ferrero and Ronald Wintrobe (eds.), *The Political Economy of Theocracy* (New York: Palgrave Macmillan, 2009), 101.

p. 74: "As the Lord lives . . ." Brigham Young, *Journal of Discourses*, Volumes 3–4 (1856), 40.

Index

Numbers in ***bold italic*** refer to captions.

Contributors

Tara Derrick has written nonfiction articles and books for young readers on a variety of topics. She also writes fiction. As a freelance editor, Tara works to help authors who write fiction for children and young adults. Tara lives in West Virginia with husband and their three children.